Kairos

New Women's Voices Series, 148

poems by

Libby Maxey

Finishing Line Press
Georgetown, Kentucky

Kairos

New Women's Voices Series, 148

Copyright © 2019 by Libby Maxey
ISBN 978-1-63534-949-8 First Edition
All rights reserved under International and Pan-American Copyright Conventions.
No part of this book may be reproduced in any manner whatsoever without written permission from the publisher, except in the case of brief quotations embodied in critical articles and reviews.

ACKNOWLEDGMENTS

With gratitude to the editors of the following journals where these poems first appeared:

3Elements Literary Review: "Onsen, Kirishima"
Brain of Forgetting: "Fieldstone Wall"
Crannóg Magazine: "Kairos"
IthacaLit: "lusus naturae"
Kestrel: "Anachronism," "In the Week After Easter"
Mezzo Cammin: "Chamber Odyssey," "Keeping on Nodding Terms"
The Mom Egg Review: "Fair Food," "As Close as Understanding"
Naugatuck River Review: "Spring comes early to the Northampton State Hospital for the insane"
Off the Coast: "Conversations in Winter," "Open Cluster"
Peacock Journal: "December," "Pas de Deux," "Homecoming"
Pinyon: "Washaway"
Stone Walls II: "At the terminus, Conway Station Rd."
Tule Review: "Starting Kindergarten"

Thanks also to Dennis Martin Piana, editor of *The Poet's Seat Contest Silver Anniversary Anthology*, where "Song for Ada MacLeish" first appeared.

Publisher: Leah Maines
Editor: Christen Kincaid
Cover Art: Astrid Erickson
Author Photo: Trent Maxey
Cover Design: Elizabeth Maines McCleavy

Printed in the USA on acid-free paper.
Order online: www.finishinglinepress.com
 also available on amazon.com

Author inquiries and mail orders:
Finishing Line Press
P. O. Box 1626
Georgetown, Kentucky 40324
U. S. A.

Table of Contents

Anachronism 1
Pas de Deux 2
Chamber Odyssey 3
Zeitgeist 4
In the sanctuary, Amherst 5
Onsen, Kirishima 6
December 7
In the Week after Easter 8
Spring comes early to the Northampton State Hospital
    for the insane 9
Wet April 10
lusus naturae 11
Fieldstone Wall 12
At the terminus, Conway Station Rd. 13
As Close as Understanding 14
Conversations in Winter 15
River St. Post Office 16
The lighthouse keeper's hours 17
Washaway 18
The Absence of Accustomed Things 19
Open Cluster 20
Starting Kindergarten 21
Fair Food 22
Song for Ada MacLeish 23
Homecoming 24
Keeping on Nodding Terms 25
Kairos 27

for my family

Anachronism

> *I do not mean to imply that I consider modern, non-metrical poetry "better" or "superior" to the great poetry of the past, which I love and honor. That would obviously be absurd. But I do feel that there are few poets today whose sensibility naturally expresses itself in the traditional forms (except for satire or pronounced irony), and that those who do so are somewhat anachronistic.*
> —Denise Levertov, "On the Function of the Line"

Perhaps I have been loved amidst the rows
Of aging gravestones, silent under trees
At night and spared, by settling in their lees,
The cover of an even skim of snow.
I sing by numbers, measured breath, each note
A contoured shape delineated by
Another for another voice to try—
Alive, I am this music's warmest coat.
Do you know all my patterns and designs?
Or how I titivate the syntax of
The moment with an heirloom comb? The spun
And snipped I carry and the threads combine.
Do you know all the ways I marry love
To my mortality? Well, here is one.

Pas de Deux

I haven't written you for much too long—
Who are you if not one who holds my words?
When you are written, you are reassured
That you are somehow still more real than wrong.
Do you not find your name is more your own
When in my hand? I let it loop and weave
With your determined wanderings relieved
In gracious space. And surely you alone
Are less so for the other name that shares
The envelope. But what were I if not
These characters in consort dancing for
Our pleasure, pretty figures, suited pairs,
A complement of lines embracing—what
If not a stately progress to your door?

Chamber Odyssey

Penelope kept busy, never sure,
But keeping faith in hand, her artful act
Of love each day the same, she would endure
The years of pushing love away—exact
Her warp and weft and smooth the shroud with which
She did conceal her heart. What did she weave
And furtively destroy by night? What rich
Depictions, true yet crafted to deceive?
What longing, what eviscerating dread,
What hope appalling, anguish unconfessed?
No vestige whispered through the finished threads,
No layered paint, no scoured palimpsest—
Propriety laid down on smothered fire—
To leave a telling shadow of desire.

Zeitgeist

If pressed, we would consent to gratitude—
Give thanks for pavement, the invaluable
Support of this one square of sidewalk—rude
To mention that the next would do as well—
Or dirt, without the tidy concrete crust,
Or rock, without the cozy loam of dead
Decayed to centuries of settled dust.
We'd say *thank God for carbon* if we'd read
About it recently enough to know
That it was more than something to be taxed.
And hydrogen and oxygen—just so
They mix with the right elements. Relaxed
Associations, toxic bonds—a land
Compounding its explosions where we stand.

In the sanctuary, Amherst

The winter afternoons are as you said
And sitting in the brown unlighted church
Although there is no sound I hear the lurch
Of dying organ wind, as if it bled
Out just before I came. Out through the flues
And thin-slit reeds, the rigid mouths gave up
Their unmade music; cancelled breaths corrupt
However many hundred leaden avenues
Above. So with this host of ciphers I
Sit waiting and the seconds each expire.
We are a cold geography, not so
Specific to this emptiness. The high
Pipes cluster sharply and the low aspire
And none of us will speak before I go.

Onsen, Kirishima

What have we done? We came away to be
together in a winter mountain's mouth
by night, to talk with all the urgency
of people cooking in the same small pot.
The slippery stone, the clouded liquor bronzed
with slivers of the roiling underground,
my silver ring—I didn't think, I saw
too late—so quickly tarnished sulfur brown.
What is the measure of this water, sold
to soothe and heal and bond by naked shock?
Our cleaving is the island's balance; old
and trembling on its bed of molten rock,
it sighs its someday shifts through steaming veins.
We dry each other, rub away the stains.

December

Forgotten fruit, a winter crown of these
Unfallen apples on the leafless trees:
They did not shy from ripening, from sheen
And russet bloom, from living fairest though
They shriveled where they sweetened; now serene,
As all the dormant things, embalmed in snow.
Spent ornaments, no wisdom would defend
The fruitless weight these frozen twigs suspend.
My reason is as meaningless as dark,
As sinking chill or rising day or small
Rough promises of pink beneath the bark.
To bear and to be borne, still borne, is all:
No lustrous purpose in the lingering red,
The silent staying of the stubborn dead.

In the Week After Easter

This wind has no white lilies on its tongue,
Nor yet a flame, but smoke—the air incensed
With last year's dead: the apple tree it wrung
In half, the ravaged lilacs, dear expense
Without reward; the wrong partitions torn.
The leaves are bickering relics in the street;
The wizened fields, a weathered skin too worn
To hold another spring. So we complete
Despair's consuming ouroboros. Who
Believes in wholeness with his bones between
His teeth? We want to force our fingers through
The wounds to find a pulse amidst our spleen
As we go mumbling winter's shibboleth—
In April's mouth November's sour breath.

Spring comes early to the Northampton State Hospital for the insane

So many robins convalescing on
The wet brown lawns, these wormy pleasure grounds
Below the iridescent slates, along
The spreading red brick wings. The fog around
The feathered sycamores and over—through
The portico, an exhalation from
The earth's small passages, the down of new
And airy nests on every sill. Nostrum.
Today there might be music—parlor songs—
The lessons of a former life unlocked
In keys that cannot change: their action as
A padded hammer striking tightly drawn
And pinblocked wires inside a wooden box,
Appoggiaturas fluttering at the glass.

Wet April
Aberdeen, Washington

Still waiting for the leaves. The apple boughs,
A fleet of curving keels long barnacled
With bone-white lichen in the sea foam moss,
Lie anchored in the flooded pasture. Cows
Drift up below to scratch their matted, dull
Black coats. Slight wood for such weight, well embossed
By winters. Patient orchard: these the roots
The spreading river left, pulling back
And forth with turning on the harbor tides,
Unmooring. This the trunk still dreaming fruit.
Young horsetails cluster, feathered lime and stacked
With stripes, new-made for currents such as glide
The coral of the gold antipodes—
Bright sprays of rippling fish for sun-warmed seas.

lusus naturae

No work today. The plows, at 2 p.m.,
Still haven't done a thing. Meanwhile the dog
Has riffled, snuffling, every drifted hem
Of tree and tussock, every sheltering log;
The boys have shoveled, mounded, rolled; and we
Have read the things we meant to read last week
And walked the unwalked fields and woods and seen
The baffled daffodils beneath this freak
Of April. Humbling, lovely, how a touch
Of unexpected air's a season's lapse.
What's unambiguously good? Not much.
Not I. But I give thanks for what, perhaps,
Ought not to be but is, unscheduled sport
And worldly living of a different sort.

Fieldstone Wall

Clumsy, stilted tessellation, moss
For mortar, brooding foxes in the gaps;
The cows recline against and strain across
And snow unsettles, pries by stealth. Perhaps
The leaves are comfort and the press of brush
A touch, a consolation. Are the roots
That heave beneath companions? Is the crush
Of leaning trunks, the scrape of sprouting shoots
Akin to an embrace? Decrepit pile,
Near useless aggregation near collapse,
What hard conviction steadies all the while
An incidental unloved thing? Perhaps
Endurance is an acquiescence to
A softer edge, a slant, a greener hue.

At the terminus, Conway Station Rd.

Bronze river, shivered silver over rocks
Stone ruins at the edges—broken teeth,
Hard bread—old trestle footings growing trees.
They knew the town was real when there were rails
Across the water, wine-dark boxcars packed
With cargo—lumber, cotton, tin and shoes,
Tool handles, apples, cattle, sheep and milk—
And people bound for distant ports. Above
The wooded bank—the other bank—there's still
The scraping, churning hurry of the cars,
The city sound of going somewhere else.
Below, smooth-skimming leaves shape roiling blooms
Of tiny steel-backed fish; they seed their thin
Iron shadows on the bottom—live black sparks.

As Close as Understanding

I said I understood, and it was true
As far as narrow understanding goes.
A sightless leech and small, it only knows
The compass of its mouth, the feel of you
Just there, just then, the spot of skin it drew,
The bit of blood it raised before it fell
Away, the mouth still gaping—not to tell,
But straining to take hold again. Too few
The days when it might find you waiting, still,
The water past your waist, exposed but for
The modesty of shadows—now restore
That slim yet certain seal, and now refill
The guessing space with present verity
To reassure me that I almost see.

Conversations in Winter

If what I heard were darkling sleet, a nick
As soon forgotten as perceived upon
My cheek, a touch of frozen sky, a prick
That skin's own warmth absorbs—now felt, now gone—
I wouldn't look for culprits in the drifts
By day or watch the snowflakes on my sleeve
For sharper points or microscopic rifts
Between the fated crystals. To retrieve
Each word embedded in my flesh and hold
The icy shards out flat to classify
And map a meaning in the shifting cold
Is winter work. If I could set it by,
Your eyes were radiant waters of the south
And Lethe were the moisture of your mouth.

River St. Post Office

As unremarkable as asphalt, this
Our one-room outpost of bureaucracy—
Except that once there was a spreading tree
Out front, the sort enshrined elsewhere. Each gliss
Of swithering breeze might have been prophecy,
Dodonian wisdom, here among the leaves
The susurrous secrets of the building's eaves,
The rushes in the swales, the distant sea.
We'd pull around beneath its canopy
And slip our sacred papers through the slot,
An ancillary mouth, entrusting there
No offerings to sylvan deity
But only checks and forms, each mortal jot
Assuring fate it was our own affair.

The lighthouse keeper's hours
Grays Harbor Light Station, 1889

One hundred thirty-five steps. The light
Revolving red and white, a shell of glass
Afloat in mercury, requires a can
Of kerosene twelve times a day. So tight
The curve of oyster-colored iron, I pass
The same point seven times each way, a hand
Clicking circles in the ocean's clock.
I climb. The weight descends as if to sound
The depth of this dim nautilus. The lives
Of men at sea hang by the ropes and by
My heaving, climbing, pouring, turning round
The vents to keep the soot at bay and block
The gales. Above, the lantern sails; below
The steady flash, my steady to and fro.

Washaway
    North Cove, Washington

This beach town, going south these hundred years
And more, another sweep of bricks and beams
With every storm—grand houses one by one
Made shipwreck. Cannery gone, disappeared
By night; for days the coastguard station seemed
To float beyond the cliff above undone
Foundations; pine and spruce and lighthouse fell
Together; foxgloved gardens slid away
Behind the drifting sections of hotel,
The ragged hall. The dead, at least, were saved.
The view gets better, too, from windows still
On shore,
        for now,
                however long,
                        until

The Absence of Accustomed Things

I saw it, but to speak of it, to claim
It real, to challenge it I did not dare,
As if in speaking I should curse the name
Of some divinity. I could not bear
To scorn a thing ineffable with lips
And tongue, to point, to stare, to crave.
I thought of other things. Thus we eclipse
Politely that which we would die to save.
Departure is a disconcerting hiss
From somewhere; something somehow disappears—
An undetected aperture—remiss
We were, but how is even now unclear.
The absence of accustomed things, the lack
Inordinate keeps breathing at our backs.

Open Cluster

Where there is so much love, it strains the strings
Of kindness. Amplitude increases with
Embraces and admonishment and rings
That band and bind us swell and test the myth
That care coheres and gathers in. Each day
A struggle in a star, each word exchanged
A nova. Blinded by our light our way
We burn, more knowing kindred, more estranged.
How soon after the silence of the womb
The tensions that anticipated birth
Are drawn. How soon our universe expands
In tenderness and rage. How quick they bloom
And spark, how great their magnitude, their worth.
In some dark nebula I take their hands.

Starting Kindergarten

I know what it was like, your very first
Day. Obviously. You're not my oldest child.
I know you didn't drink your milk; plain thirst
Was never stronger than your whim. The wild,
Frenetic tarantelle was not a part
Of the curriculum. The homework, you
Devised—you were not asked to honor art
With further studies in the series, "View
Of Robot Wars With Extra Guns." I know
This keen enthusiasm for a half-
Imagined thing, the pricking, pushy joy
Of making what is dully given glow.
While you were gone, I ate pâté; the staff
Admired my hat; I savored one less boy.

Fair Food

The children said they saw you as we stood
In line. I heard you then, explaining, calm,
Your measured conversation plain and good
Like cooling bread, an apple on your palm
Outstretched, a table set for autumn with
A cloth and cotton napkins on the left.
Such clean, inviting words—no bitter pith,
No blemished shell, no disconcerting heft.
Our scalding, fried indulgence now in hand,
I turned and watched you as we found a place
To perch and share one plate three ways. Behind
The crowd you moved away in silence bland
And insufficient, hunger in your face,
Your downward glance like biting at the rind.

Song for Ada MacLeish

I heave the stroller uphill, uphill, steep
The rubber singing and my arms like staves.
Five months along, no music in the strain
And searing lungs, no beauty in the fear
But mad to keep from tipping back, to keep
The self that holds the stage with grace and saves
A thought for diction—now teetering again
Outside my tessitura. You were here
On rougher roads than I, in colder years,
Who once beguiled soirées, before the trees
And turkeys, children, guests in hills remote;
With no one home from which to disappear,
You held to voice and breath and memory—
When *Clair de lune* was supple in your throat.

Homecoming

I do not dream the wedding cakes of those
Who have not learned to tie their shoes, no more
Than I anticipate the ebbs and flows
Of feeling on my heart's dark-patterned shore.
Arrival is a word I wait on, not
A vision of my expectation. Come
And be with me; the way it is is just
How it should be. I know you will have brought
The story with you. We will be the sum
Of all that longing might imagine: trust,
The value of each variable term.
Come run yourself aground where we have made
Our shifting bar beneath the currents; trade
Your ship for sea and we will find it firm.

Keeping on Nodding Terms

> *I think we are well advised to keep on nodding terms with the people we used to be, whether we find them attractive company or not.*
> —*Joan Didion, "On Keeping a Notebook"*

1.

Thoughts on Nietzsche During Palm Sunday Mass
   Age 18

You say I worship hatred's progeny,
And see in every act of Christian love
The work of selfish hands in selfless gloves.
Too well I know my own duplicity.
You scorn my humble penitence and damn
The self-inflicted wounds by which I gain
The masochistic pleasure of my pain
To compensate for loathing what I am.
It sickens you to contemplate the ills
That I have made my own. But I am sick
At them as well. I long to justify
The weakness which condemns what nature wills,
But sink beneath my guilt, now doubly thick,
And prove your words in wanting to deny.

2.

Thoughts for My 18-Year-Old Self
    Age 38

Two decades spent and still we write our verse
Epistles to these second persons who
Do not collect their mail. I'll reimburse
You with these lines for all their overdue
Replies. Since Nietzsche wouldn't, I'll applaud
Your will to power. No mawkish counterpoise,
No teenage bluster sure of its reward,
No playbook bluff in someone else's voice;
Just knowing all the pieces on the board.
I wonder, could I write you better now
Than you did then? There'd be a little more
Enjambment, certainly. But shame, and how
You peel it, seed it, cut it from the core
And smooth it through a literary mill
Would be the same: I am your codicil.

Kairos

Then I will go to you, my dear ordeal,
Across the burning ploughshares, radiant coals—
Whatever fire my bare and blameless soles
Shall tread will be the hearth at which I kneel,
Attending Hestia's rites. I give my bones,
Still tightly wrapped, in offering, but they
Remain my own, to walk again the way
I came, retrieving all your boiling stones.
What love, my stubborn hand, my hand, my proof—
A sturdy blanket for the searing iron.
Coins for Charon, Orphean strings, the lyre
Upraised across my palm will be the roof
That shelters us this side the underworld:
I choose our passage, pay with fingers furled.

Additional Acknowledgments

I am most grateful to Leah Maines and Finishing Line Press for honoring me with the New Women's Voices chapbook prize, and for seeing this, my first *libellus*, into being. I appreciate my community of colleagues at *Literary Mama* and Marjorie Altman Tesser at *Mom Egg Review*, who make the world a better place for mother writers, including this one. I also appreciate the teachers who have improved my thinking and writing over the years, including Doc Carter, Tess Gallagher, and Dana Burgess, for whose class I wrote the first half of "Keeping on Nodding Terms" my freshman year of college. Special thanks go to all my writer (and reader) friends on whose support, insight, and good taste I rely, and without whose interest and encouragement this collection would not exist. I am especially indebted to Joanne Clarkson, Rebecca Hart Olander, Jean Blakeman, Sharon Tracy, Adin Thayer, Beth Filson, Graham Christian, Anna Smith, Jim Mead, Joseph Smeall-Villaroel, Christine Stewart-Nuñez, and Linda McCullough Moore. I am also grateful to my family—to my niece Astrid, who donated her art to the cover; to my parents, Glenn and Dotty, and siblings, Ian and Hilary, with whom I enjoyed a mutually creative upbringing; and to Trent, Amory and Henry, who take it for granted that this work is a reasonable use of my time.

Libby Maxey has a BA in English from Whitman College and an MA in medieval studies from Cornell University. She is a senior editor at the online journal *Literary Mama*, where she has been a part of the Literary Reflections department since 2012. She also edits for Amherst College and as a freelancer (libbymaxey.com). She has won both the Poet's Seat Poetry Contest and the Robert P. Collén Poetry Contest, and her work was selected for the Northampton Arts Council's 2017 Visual Arts and Poetry Biennial. Her poems have appeared in several anthologies and in various journals, online and in print, including *Pirene's Fountain, The Fourth River, Emrys, Think,* and *Common Ground Review*. She reviews others' poetry for *The Mom Egg Review* and *Solstice*. Her nonliterary activities include singing classical repertoire and mothering two sons. She lives with her family in Western Massachusetts.

www.ingramcontent.com/pod-product-compliance
Lightning Source LLC
LaVergne TN
LVHW041512070426
835507LV00012B/1514